GLOBAL INDUST

UNCOVERED

THE FOOD INDUSTRY

ROB BOWDEN

WAYLAND

First published in 2009 by Wayland

Copyright © Wayland 2009

Wayland
338 Euston Road
London NW1 3BH

Wayland Australia
Level 17/207 Kent Street
Sydney NSW 2000

Series Editor: Claire Shanahan
Editor: Susie Brooks
Consultant: Steph Warren
Designer: Rebecca Painter
Picture Researcher: Rob Bowden
Proofreader and indexer: Hayley Fairhead

British Library Cataloguing in Publication Data
 Bowden, Rob, 1973-
   The food industry. -- (Global industries uncovered)
   1. Food industry and trade--Juvenile literature.
   2. Industrial location--Juvenile literature.
   3. Globalization--Economic aspects--Juvenile
literature.
   I. Title II. Series
   338.4'7664-dc22

ISBN 978 0 7502 5829 6

Printed in Malaysia

Picture acknowledgements:
Cover and p13 © Danny Lehman/CORBIS; 6 © Martin
Rogers/CORBIS; 7, 9, 14, 17, 20, 26, 31 © EASI-
Images/Rob Bowden; 11 © EASI-Images/Jenny
Matthews; 19 © EASI-Images/Adrian Cooper, 34 ©
EASI-Images/Ed Parker, 37 © EASI-Images/Miguel
Hunt;12 © Peter Dench/Peter Dench/Corbis; 22 ©
Andrew Holbrooke/Corbis; 25 Greg Balfour
Evans/Alamy; 27 Paul Glendell/Alamy; 28 © Fred de
Noyelle/Godong/Corbis; 29 Jeffrey Blackler/ Alamy; 32
© doc-stock/Corbis; 33 © Kena Betancur/
epa/Corbis; 35 © Carlos Cazalis/Corbis; 38 Nick Turner/
Alamy; 39 © Joel W. Rogers/Corbis; 41
BrazilPhotoscom/Alamy

Wayland is a division of Hachette Children's Books,
an Hachette UK company.
www.hachette.co.uk

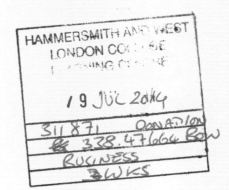
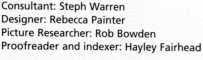

Contents

CASE STUDIES
UNCOVERED

As the snow lay thick on the ground outside the kitchen window, Ella chopped a banana to add to her cereal for breakfast. Her dad was enjoying his coffee and her mum her tea. Her older brother Kai was making his packed lunch with rice and beans and many different vegetables. It was Ella's birthday today, so tonight they were going out for a surprise meal. As Ella wondered what they would eat, she was completely unaware of the complicated global industry behind the food she and her family enjoyed. Many of us are the same: we enjoy an incredible range of foods but have little idea about where they come from, how they are grown and made, or who is involved in the process.

The global food industry

A global industry is one that operates (designs, manufactures, sells, etc) in many different countries and continents. Because of this, global industries can connect people around the world, often in ways that the individuals who are part of them are unaware of. Ella's dad, for example, probably has little idea of what life is like for the coffee growers who produce the beans he enjoys in his coffee each morning. And yet the connections between the different parts of a global industry such as food are very important. They involve political, social, cultural and environmental issues and can have a dramatic impact on some people. The pickers who supplied Ella with her breakfast banana, for example, are paid so little in some countries that they cannot afford to send their own children to school or even give them a proper breakfast.

Many of us have little connection with people on the other side of the world who work to produce many of the foods we enjoy. This banana picker is in Costa Rica.

Globalisation: a shrinking world

Globalisation means that we live in a smaller, more connected, more interdependent world. Physically, the world is not smaller, but it feels smaller because we have access to more of it. Geographical distances seem nearer because it takes less time now to travel to them or communicate between them. This has been made possible by improvements in technology. Mobile phones, the internet, low-cost flights and cheaper cars are all examples of this. Global connections are faster, easier and cheaper, which means that industries use them more. It can be easy for those living in more developed countries (MDCs) to take this for granted, but the technological revolution has not taken place at the same rate all over the world. As a result, some countries have benefited more than others from globalisation.

These people are enjoying coffee in an Italian-branded café in South Korea. The coffee they are drinking was most likely grown in South America, East Africa or Indonesia, and processed in Europe. It is just one example of the complex links in what is now a global food industry.

A long history

Many of the food products we consider traditional to our own cultures, in fact have a long global history. Potatoes – considered a staple food in many countries – have their origins in Peru, for example. Spanish explorers brought potatoes to Europe in 1536 and they then spread across the world through European traders. Coffee, tea, rice, beans, tomatoes, onions and chocolate have similar global histories.

The world on your plate

Improved storage technology (refrigeration, freezing, etc) and transportation means that food is today a more global industry than ever. 'Fresh apples' on sale in your local supermarket may have been picked ten months earlier, and on the other side of the world. The movement of people through migration, business and tourism has also contributed to an increasingly globalised industry by creating an increasingly multi-cultural diet around the world. Indian and Chinese food is popular in a wide range of countries, for example, as are American-style burgers and fried chicken.

Global impacts

Analysing a typical family meal in Europe or North America today can involve a global journey to several countries and cover thousands of miles. This may allow consumers to eat fresh produce in the middle of winter or enjoy foods that don't grow where they live, but what does it mean at the other end of the connection? It can be positive, providing farmers with new markets and a good income. Farmers in Kenya, for example, benefit from selling vegetables to Europe, but there is a negative side. Some of those 'export' vegetables are grown on land that once produced food for Kenya and this has led to food shortages in local markets.

There are also human rights and environmental issues linked to food production, such as the long hours and poor pay of many workers in the global food industry and the clearance of tropical rainforests to graze beef cattle or grow soya beans in Brazil. Global challenges such as climate change have been linked to food production too, as it is one of the biggest users of energy and a major contributor to the build-up of greenhouse gases in the atmosphere.

The food corporations

As the food industry has globalised it has also become more corporate. Local farmers selling in local markets to local people are a vanishing reality. Instead, supermarket chains and giant food companies buy from farmers (or even own the farms themselves) and process, package and distribute the food to their stores and outlets around the globe. Some of these food companies are among the largest businesses in the world, and are known as transnational companies (TNCs). They are able to use their size to exert great pressure on producers and consumers, thus controlling the supply and demand of the food that ends up on our plates.

> *Air-freighted fruit and vegetables are a bad habit that our supermarket chains have cultivated among ...consumers. They have actively encouraged the idea that it is entirely reasonable for us to expect to be able to buy every fruit and vegetable produced anywhere on the planet, 365 days of the year.*
>
> Joanna Blythman, author of *Shopped – the Shocking Power of British Supermarkets*, 2005

Globalisation has led to increasingly varied diets and food styles. This is especially true in MDCs. This Chinese restaurant is in London. Similar restaurants can today be found in towns and cities across the world.

Locating the global food industry

There are few parts of the world that are not somehow touched by the modern global food industry, but its activities (production and consumption) are more concentrated in some countries and regions than others. Consumption is greatest in MDCs, and lowest in the least developed regions of the world. Comparing the average daily calorie intake of countries is one way to see this difference (see table opposite). This shows us that an average person living in the USA consumes twice the daily calories of the average Ethiopian.

Production is more mixed. Countries have traditionally produced foods suited to their particular environments (climate, soil type, rainfall, etc). New technologies such as heated greenhouses, agricultural chemicals and irrigation mean that these traditional barriers are less important. Heated greenhouses can produce vegetables out of season, and irrigation and chemicals allow previously unfarmed land to be cultivated. In addition, plant science has introduced new varieties of crops that are suited to growing in conditions that were previously unsuited to growing crops. Spain and Israel, for example, are two countries that have greatly increased their production of fruit and vegetables using a combination of irrigation, greenhouses and new plant varieties. As food production has become more scientific and technological, it is the large companies and wealthier MDCs that have dominated production. Even food grown in less developed countries (LDCs) is often exported to MDCs in raw form and then processed and sold by companies based there.

SPOTLIGHT

Taking advantage

Some of the biggest companies in the global food industry use their wealth and power to take advantage of the opportunities of globalisation. They can produce in many countries at once to make the most of different climates at different times of the year. They can also switch production from place to place, according to where the costs are lowest. Producing food uses a lot of energy (much of it using fossil fuels) and can be very labour intensive, so cost is an important factor. Finding low-cost places to produce food is good for the companies and delivers cheap food for their consumers, but in some countries it can mean low wages for workers and very poor working conditions.

A global phenomenon

In 2008, the price of many key foods increased dramatically and led to riots in several less developed regions of the world. Experts warned that this was the start of a global food crisis. They claimed that it was not possible to keep producing cheap food and that the global system was unfair and needed to change. In 2008, up to a billion people around the world went to bed hungry each night because of food shortages. Most of these were in poorer less developed regions. At the same time, there were record levels of obesity among people living in more developed regions. Food for many people in MDCs is no longer a means of surviving, but is taken for granted. Food has become like fashion with its own trends, seasons, television shows and celebrity chefs. It is a truly global phenomenon, but it is also a global problem.

These people at a feeding station in Sudan are among the many millions of people in the world who continue to suffer from hunger despite living in a world that has more food than at any time in history.

Average daily calorie intake per person	
COUNTRY/REGION	(kcal/person/day)
USA	3,770
Ireland	3,690
France	3,640
Canada	3,590
Germany	3,490
Denmark	3,450
UK	3,440
South Africa	2,940
China	2,940
World	2,800
India	2,440
Thailand	2,410
Bangladesh	2,200
Kenya	2,150
Ethiopia	1,860

This table shows the average number of calories consumed daily by each person in a selection of countries. It demonstrates the inequality that exists in access to food around the world. [Source: UN FAO, 2007]

Connections within the global food industry span the world and link people, governments and countries together in complex ways. This interdependence extends beyond the food industry itself, however, and relates to other industries too. The advertising industry, for example, is closely linked to food products and mainstream media such as television, radio and magazines also has a large amount of its content linked to food issues. Transportation is another industry that is closely connected to food. Airlines, shipping companies and road haulage firms all rely heavily on the food industry for business. In the UK, the food industry accounts for around 25 per cent of all goods transported by road.

Culture of dependency

Within the food industry there are many people who have become almost entirely dependent on others for their livelihoods. This pattern is often highly unequal, with larger companies and wealthier countries having great influence over smaller companies and poorer countries. Supermarket chains who wish to offer their customers low-priced food are able to shop around between different suppliers and pay lower prices. They can do this because in countries like the UK and USA they account for the majority of all food sales. If farmers or small food companies want to sell their produce to these powerful supermarkets, they have to accept their prices and other terms or risk losing business as the supermarkets will simply go elsewhere. Investigations into these relationships have shown that if suppliers stand up to the supermarkets, they may sometimes run the risk of being de-listed as a supplier.

A worker stacks shelves in a Tesco store. The buying power of large supermarkets like this has reduced prices for shoppers, but has not always been good for producers.

Vulnerable farmers

Small-scale farmers in LDCs are among the most vulnerable of all those involved in the food industry. They are often paid very little for their produce and may have little guarantee that it will be bought at all. In addition, they often sell their produce in raw form. This means that they do not benefit from the higher price consumers will pay for the processed product – this added value benefits the companies and retailers in MDCs.

These workers are harvesting peppers grown on large farms in New Mexico, USA. Many of the vegetables that we buy in supermarkets are harvested on similar large-scale farms.

PERSPECTIVES FOR DEBATE

"Having travelled to many countries to meet farmers it was very clear that supermarkets treated all farmers equally – unfortunately that is equally badly and it was the name of Tesco which came up time and time again. If we are to have a future as farmers and sustainable agriculture then we need to control supermarket power."

Michael Hart, Chairman of Small and Family Farms Alliance, 2004

"We do not believe that exploitative relationships with suppliers could ensure the quality, reliability and product development that our customers demand. We favour long-term relationships over short-term deals. We seek to get the best value from our suppliers so that we can pass this on to our customers, but we seek to do this in a fair way which reflects the costs our suppliers face. We need strong, dynamic and confident suppliers. Our success is tied to theirs."

Tesco plc website, 2009

Food and rural change

Food is now produced on an enormous scale. Farms have become bigger and machines now do jobs that were previously carried out by skilled farmers. Many of the jobs are now unskilled and can be done by anyone. Many are also seasonal, such as fruit picking, and are done by casual labourers who move to follow the work. These shifts in production have led to dramatic changes in many rural areas. Communities that once relied on farming have seen their populations fall as machines replace people and force them to migrate to towns and cities to find new jobs. In 1950, around 71 per cent of the world's people lived and worked in rural areas, but today that has fallen to less than 50 per cent. In more developed regions, fewer than 25 per cent of people live in rural areas today.

These people are casual labourers harvesting grapes in the vineyards of South East Australia. They are typical of many unskilled workers who now dominate food production and have contributed to great changes in rural economies across the world.

Changes on the high street

Linked to the increased industrialisation of farming are changes in how food is sold on the high street. The growth of large supermarket chains, often in out-of-town locations, has led to the closure of many small and independent food shops that cannot compete with low supermarket prices. Many towns have lost independent bakers, butchers and grocers, for example, and some have none at all. These changes are linked to changing work patterns in many countries where people (and especially women) are working more and so are less able to devote the time to shop in several independent stores. Supermarkets, many of which are open late at night or even 24 hours at day, provide a convenient 'one-stop shop' for such busy lifestyles.

SPOTLIGHT

Hunger in a world of plenty

The global food industry now produces more food than at any time in history — more than one-and-a-half times what is needed to provide every human being with a healthy diet. And yet up to a billion people around the world are going hungry, so what is going wrong? Many experts say it is not the supply of food that is the problem, but the distribution of food. Trading laws and the power of large companies mean that food is transported from Africa or Asia to Europe and North America only to be wasted and thrown away, whilst some of those who produced it suffer from persistently empty stomachs. Many people consider that hunger in a world of plenty is unjust and are calling for changes in the global food industry.

The microwave society

Societies themselves have changed as a result of the global food industry. Food science has found ways to store and pre-prepare food for quick cooking and consumption. The microwave oven allows foods that once took an hour to cook to be ready in just a couple of minutes. Processed foods that suit this new style of cooking and eating have grown in popularity over the last 20 years and today make up a considerable proportion of food sales.

The problem is that in order to make and preserve these foods, high levels of salt, sugars and fat are used and these are bad for our health. They are linked to heart disease, strokes and cancers and to an increase in overweight populations. The World Health Organisation (WHO) report that over a billion people in the world are now overweight with some 300 million clinically obese. This creates enormous costs for governments and health services. In the UK, the National Health Service (NHS) spends an estimated £1 billion every year on obesity-related problems. The cost of obesity to the UK economy as a whole is over £2 billion per year.

> These [opposing] poles of the global food economy, obesity and hunger, reflect the basic reality that while food is elemental to life and health it is conceived as a commodity and not a right...and the motive force of profit prevails over concerns about equity and nutrition.

Tony Weis, author of The Global Food Economy, 2007

Harvesting the planet

Food production has a major impact on the health and sustainability of natural environments. It is a prime user of energy and water, and each year vast areas of land are cleared to create new farmland. Many practices, for example the use of chemicals such as fertilisers and pesticides to encourage crop growth or kill weeds, also cause damage. These impacts are not just felt on land. Fishing fleets today go further and catch more fish than ever before, and in many parts of the world the oceans have almost been emptied by years of commercial over-fishing.

As the world's population continues to expand (by an estimated 1.5 billion people by 2025) and demands even more food, the pressures on the environment are set to increase further. Many environmentalists believe that we have already stretched the planet too far and need to drastically alter our diets and food production to find a more sustainable way to feed ourselves.

The hidden, or 'virtual', water in our food	
Product (quantity)	**Litres of water**
Milk (per litre)	1,000
Bread (per slice of white bread)	40
Tea (per cup)	30
Coffee (per cup)	410
Beef (per kg)	15,500
Hamburger (per regular hamburger)	2,400
Apple (per apple)	70
Orange (per orange)	50
Rice (per kg)	3,400
Soybeans (per kg)	1,800

Source: Water Footprint Network

Water – the key to everything

Water is essential for survival – all living things require it. Producing food is a thirsty business and agriculture accounts for around 70 per cent of global water use. The processing of food uses yet more, and so by the time a meal lands on your plate it can hide a phenomenal amount of water usage (see table). This is significant in global terms because when food is exported between countries, it is also this hidden water that is being exported and therefore not available for local use. Many environmental experts believe that hidden water use is one of the biggest problems facing increased food production and that it will become worse as people's diets around the world become more meat-based.

This table shows how much water is needed to produce a variety of popular food products.

SPOTLIGHT

Vegetarian versus meat diet

An average meat-based diet consumes over twice the water and several times the energy of a vegetarian diet, because of the water and energy used by rearing the animals we eat. The difference is even higher if that diet includes a high proportion of processed meats or processed foods that contain meat. Many global food corporations make greater profit from meat-based products and so actively promote such a diet. This has led to a dramatic increase in the amount of meat consumed worldwide, from 100 million tonnes in 1970 to around 234 million tonnes by 2003. Current trends suggest it will almost double again by 2050 to around 460 million tonnes. Much of this increase is expected to come from countries such as China and India, which have large populations and have historically had a more vegetarian diet.

> *The human appetite for animal flesh is a driving force behind virtually every major category of environmental damage now threatening the human future: deforestation, erosion, fresh water scarcity, air and water pollution, climate change, biodiversity loss, social injustice, the destabilisation of communities and the spread of disease.*

Worldwatch Institute, Washington, USA, 2008

These women are weeding a rice paddy field in southern India. Like many food processes, rice production has a major impact on the environment, especially through water use.

It all looks the same!

One of the criticisms of the global food industry is that it is reducing choice and driving us all towards a diet that is more or less the same no matter where we are in the world. This happens because it is cheaper for the large companies that control much of the industry to produce the same products for several different markets rather than adapt them to different cultures or tastes. McDonald's restaurants, for example, serve their particular brand of food to 52 million people a day across more than 100 countries. This kind of standardisation of our diets is being mirrored by other global brands, as shown in the table below.

This table shows the size and spread of some of the best-known high street brands in the world, based on the company websites in February 2009. How many of these names feature in your local town?

Global food brands			
Brand	Countries	Outlets	Customers (daily)
McDonald's	> 100	> 30,000	> 52 million
Burger King	> 69	> 11,200	> 11 million
KFC	> 80	> 11,000	approx 8 million
Starbucks	44	15,756	no data
Coca-Cola	> 200	> 90,500	1.5 billion

Knowing what we want

Those concerned about the spread of global brands state that they are removing choice for the consumer. This is sometimes through competition, such as a Pizza Hut or Starbucks replacing the local pizzeria or coffee shop – but it is also through advertising.

Many global food companies spend millions of dollars on advertising (McDonald's spend an estimated US$2 billion annually) to convince us to try their products, tempting us with offers, deals and even toys. It is effective too, and is changing the eating habits of billions of people. China, for example, had hardly any Western fast food restaurants until KFC and Pizza Hut opened in 1987. McDonald's followed in 1990 and by the end of 2008 they had well over 3,500 restaurants between them.

Too much choice?

Another perspective on the global food industry is that we now have too much choice! Supermarkets now stock more products from more countries than ever before and the range of restaurants on our high streets is expanding all the time. Indian, Chinese, Italian, Thai, Japanese, Mexican, French and Spanish restaurants are now commonplace in even quite small towns around the world. In large cities the choice is enormous. The problem, say critics, is that this choice is not all it seems, but is in many cases a sanitised choice – traditional cuisine that has been adapted for a mass market so that it can be mass produced for maximum profits. The Indian meal you think you are enjoying could be far removed from the genuine thing.

> People have been eating since the beginning of time. But they've only been eating Chicken McNuggets since 1983. Fast food is a recent invention. During the last thirty years fast food has spread from the United States to every corner of the globe.
>
> Eric Schlosser and Charles Wilson, authors of *Chew on This*, 2006

A billboard in Beijing advertises Nescafé coffee – one of the many brands to have achieved almost global recognition. For many global food brands, China in particular is a new and fast-growing market.

The global food corporation: power in food

Most people have heard of McDonald's. In fact, their trademark golden arches are said to be more recognised worldwide than the Christian cross. But McDonald's are relatively small in the larger global food industry. The really big players are the agricultural and food TNCs. Some of these are little known to everyday consumers. They hide behind a whole family of brands that sometimes stretch to hundreds of different products. We might recognise these from the supermarket shelves, but it is the corporate boardrooms behind them where the real action takes place.

This table shows the ten largest food corporations in the world in 2008.

The ten largest food corporations in the world			
Company	Country	Sales (US$ billion)	Rank (in top 2,000 global companies)
Wal-Mart Stores	USA	378.8	16
Nestlé	Switzerland	94.76	45
Altria Group	USA	38.05	88
Unilever	Netherlands/UK	54.82	94
Coca-Cola	USA	28.86	123
PepsiCo	USA	39.47	131
Kraft Foods	USA	37.24	153
InBev	Belgium	21.07	191
Archer Daniels	USA	52.92	212
Diageo	UK	15.02	254

Source: Forbes, 2009

These Masai warriors at a rural market in southern Kenya stand in front of a store promoting soft drinks from the global drinks giant, Coca-Cola. Even the most remote parts of the world are not out of reach for the world's largest global food companies.

The hourglass model

The easiest way to understand how the global food industry operates is to think of an hourglass (see below). This shows producers (farmers) at one side of the hourglass and consumers (shoppers) at the other. In between these, at the point where the hourglass becomes thinner, are the many companies that control and take part in the stages in between, such as supplying, manufacturing, buying and selling. It is these stages that are increasingly controlled by a smaller and smaller number of companies. Companies bring these stages together through vertical or horizontal integration (see Spotlight) and in doing so take greater control and have greater power over the entire industry.

Farmers/producers	3,200,000
Suppliers	160,000
Semi-manufacturers	80,000
Manufacturers	8,600
Buying desks	110
Supermarket formats	600
Outlets	170,000
Customers	89,000,000
Consumers	160,000,000

SPOTLIGHT

Vertical and horizontal integration

Companies can expand into new areas of their industry by growing vertically or horizontally. This is known as integration. Vertical integration is when a company takes greater control of more stages of the production chain. It may seek to control not just the manufacture of food, for example, but also the growing of the raw ingredients and the sale of the finished product. A company can do this by expanding, but more often it will buy or merge with other companies already in those roles. Horizontal integration is when a company seeks to control a greater share of a particular section of the industry by buying or merging with others. In the UK, for example, the Morrisons and Safeway supermarket chains merged to form the UK's fourth-biggest supermarket group. The US supermarket giant Wal-Mart is another company that expanded in this way, by buying the UK chain ASDA in 1999. The benefit to companies of such integration is that they gain greater control of the production process, or more buying power by becoming a bigger share of the market.

A global food TNC: Nestlé

Nestlé is the largest food and drinks company in the world. Its sales of almost US$97.5 billion in 2008 were worth more than the national economies of several countries, including Bangladesh, Libya, Iceland, Kenya and Vietnam. In fact, if it were a country itself, Nestlé would be the 54th-richest in the world.

A shopper looks at Nestlé products for sale in a supermarket in Bangkok, Thailand. As the largest food manufacturer in the world, Nestlé now sells its products globally.

> *We use four simple words to describe what we believe in and what we offer consumers around the world: "Good Food, Good Life".*
>
> Nestlé, in their online publication *The World of Nestlé*, 2006

A global operation

Nestlé was founded in Switzerland in 1866 by Henri Nestlé, when he developed a type of nutritional baby food. The company now has a range of over 10,000 products in more than 130 countries, selling more than a billion products every day. These are produced in some 500 factories across 80 countries and the company employs a total of around 250,000 people. Some of its better-known brands include Nescafé, Nesquik, Maggi, Buitoni, Purina, Perrier, Kit Kat and Smarties.

Nestlé's enormous size allows it to be a leader in the development of new products, too. The company has over 3,500 people from more than 50 countries working in the research and development of new brands. It spends around US$1.3 billion on research and development every year – more than any other large food corporation. The products developed by companies such as Nestlé have helped to improve the health of millions of people by incorporating essential nutrients and vitamins into many mainstream foods. These companies have also developed more specialist foods that are particularly tailored to the nutritional needs of young people, or to athletes and very active people. Some critics argue, however, that companies like Nestlé use their power to dominate the market for new products (especially in areas such as personal health) and make enormous profits for themselves as a result.

SPOTLIGHT

The Nestlé boycott

Like almost any large TNC, Nestlé has its critics, but in the case of Nestlé there has been a highly organised campaign to boycott its products since the mid-1970s. This has focused on Nestlé's promotion of baby-milk formula as an alternative to mothers' breastfeeding. The campaigners claim that this threatens the health of millions of babies and infants because their mothers do not have access to clean water or sterilised bottles in order to make up the formula food safely. Nestlé has been criticised for promoting its products without giving mothers information about the risks and for failing to advise them that breastfeeding is still the healthiest option. The boycott began in the USA, but has now spread worldwide and made Nestlé one of the most boycotted brands in the world.

High street brands: one world, one diet?

A consequence of the food industry becoming global has been the spread of big-name brands. Names such as Wal-Mart, Tesco, 7-Eleven, Pizza Hut, Burger King, KFC, Starbucks, Coca-Cola, Pepsi and McDonald's are now found across the globe. World backpackers once had to live on whatever foods they found on their travels, but today it is possible to travel virtually anywhere and find the same foods as in your own local high street.

Global networks

The widespread distribution of familiar foods has been made possible by the power of global corporations to expand their business empires into new markets. Improvements in transportation and computerised communication, combined with advertising mediums such as satellite television and the internet, have made this process easier, cheaper and faster. It is now possible for a head office in Chicago or London to control the needs of restaurants and outlets spread across an entire continent. They can control stock, monitor sales and arrange promotions at the touch of a button. These sophisticated global networks make it possible for companies to lower their costs and increase their profits, but they also make it difficult for independent companies to compete and survive.

SPOTLIGHT

The domino effect

The presence of a global food corporation in a new location often puts local alternatives out of business. A new supermarket can cause the local grocers to shut down, or the latest coffee chain may steal customers from the local café. If this happens (and it often does) then the effects can be felt much more widely too. This is because local stores often use local suppliers and local staff. Many global companies by contrast have regional or even national suppliers and merely deliver to local stores. They also often have centralised staff, certainly at management levels where important decisions are made.

'Brand bombing'

Many high street brands use competition policies that purposefully seek to control more of the market. This has been called 'brand bombing' by the writer Naomi Klein, who explores the negative impacts of global industries in her book *No Logo*. She explains how some corporations use low pricing to drive others out of the market or flood entire regions with stores until local competition is forced to close. She claims that Starbucks, for example, use a policy called 'cannibalisation' whereby they open many stores in a single town or city. As each new store opens it takes some customers (cannibalises) from one of the others, but also from the independent competition. Starbucks as a company continues to increase its market share even if sales in individual stores fall. It can also use its wealth to advertise heavily in the local area or offer promotions, further threatening independent stores. Naomi Klein says many high street brands (not just in food) follow similar policies and that this is creating uniform high streets and reduced choice.

The US-based coffee chain Starbucks is one of several global brands that has used what some consider aggressive policies to expand their control of the global market. This includes 'brand bombing' Starbucks restaurants into traditional areas such as here in the English town of Dorchester.

> *…market-driven globalisation doesn't want diversity; quite the opposite. Its enemies are national habits, local brands and distinctive regional tastes. Of course independent stores and restaurants continue to open and thrive, but more and more, these are high-end, specialty retailers in gentrified neighborhoods, while the suburbs, small towns and working-class neighborhoods get blanketed in – and blasted by – the self-replicating clones.*
>
> Naomi Klein, author of *No Logo*, 2001

The 'win-win' model

The rate of growth of many global food companies is truly staggering. At one time, Starbucks were opening a new store every day. Burger King, which opened its first stores in China during 2008, has plans for at least 300 new Chinese outlets by 2013. Around 90 per cent of these will be franchised stores with only 10 per cent being owned directly by Burger King.

Burger King, like many other global fast food brands, has expanded rapidly by using a system called franchising to open new stores.

Franchising is a system that is widely used in the food industry to support the expansion of global brands in new and existing markets. For the brand it is a win-win situation. It works by the central company providing support to the outlet – fitting out the restaurant, providing menus, promotions, stock, staff uniforms, etc – but the outlet itself being owned by the franchisee. Burger King, Pizza Hut, KFC, Starbucks and many others all promote the opportunities to become a franchisee on their websites. However, franchising in the food industry is considered by some to be high risk because food is highly perishable. Ordering the wrong quantities or getting your market wrong could be disastrous, but the parent company carries little of this risk. There are also costs as it is the franchisee that must pay the start-up expenses of finding premises, buying stock, hiring staff, etc.

The parent company benefits by taking a share of the franchisee income (as high as 20 per cent in some instances) and by, in many cases, owning the rights to sell-on the franchise. This means that a franchisee could build up a successful business earning millions of dollars, but that this increase in value would benefit the parent company, not the franchisee, if it were to be sold.

SPOTLIGHT

Internet food

A relative newcomer on the scene is internet shopping, and this has expanded rapidly in the food sector with retailers in many countries now offering online shopping with home delivery services. This allows large corporations to push their low prices into markets where they don't even have stores and further threatens local businesses. However, the internet also provides local businesses with new opportunities. Veggie-box schemes and organic food suppliers, for example, have used the internet to help them reach customers that may live some distance away. They deliver produce using weekly deliveries or the postal system.

A woman fills vegetable boxes with seasonal produce at a farm shop in the UK. The boxes will be delivered to homes in the local area as part of a home veggie-box scheme. These are growing in popularity in many countries as a convenient way of buying locally produced food.

McDonald's: a global target?

McDonald's have been singled out for criticism more than almost any other global brand and from many different directions. Environmentalists accuse the chain of destroying rainforests, and some health experts tell us the type of food it sells is contributing to making us more obese and ill. McDonald's is not the only brand accused in this way, but as the world's largest fast food retailer it has become the number one target.

These women serve food in a McDonald's restaurant in Kuala Lumpur, Malaysia. The food offered by McDonald's and similar fast food outlets is very different from the traditional Malaysian diet.

SPOTLIGHT

Global bland?

One criticism of McDonald's and other fast food chains is that they are making all food the same around the world, leading to bland and unhealthy diets. Whilst there is much evidence to support this, many such companies do attempt to adapt their menu to cater for local preferences. Here are some of the menu items in McDonald's restaurants around the world, for example:

Japan	Teriyaki Chicken Fillet-O
India	McAloo Tikki
Netherlands	Crispy Chicken Croquette Burger

The power of the media

The pressure of negative media has led McDonald's to respond to criticisms and introduce various changes. In the UK, a new website called 'make your own mind up' invites people to share their concerns and presents McDonald's side of the story. The table below shows some of the criticisms made of McDonald's and some of their responses.

The McDonald's debate	
Criticism of McDonald's	**Response by McDonald's**
Health – many items are high in fat and sugar, and the Supersize portions (larger than 'large') that were introduced in 1994 were heavily criticised in a popular film documentary.	McDonald's removed the Supersize option in 2004, the year that the film *Supersize Me* was released. They have since introduced salads, fruit and milk to their menus.
Branding – McDonald's spends millions on advertising and has been especially criticised for advertising to children, sometimes through schools.	McDonald's stopped advertising on children's report card envelopes in Florida, USA in 2008. Its adult and children's advertising often now features the healthier products.
Sourcing – McDonald's has been accused of contributing to deforestation, and of using land to grow soya and graze cattle for its products instead of growing food for local, often poor and malnourished, people.	In the UK, McDonald's sources most of its beef, as well as many other products, from British and Irish farmers. It has provided a website for the public to find out where the food comes from.
Waste – McDonald's products are all sold in disposable containers, and the drinks use plastic straws, creating huge amounts of waste.	McDonald's sponsors council litter bins and runs its UK delivery fleet on used cooking oil.

This McDonald's restaurant in London, UK is decorated in the chain's new style. McDonald's have re-branded many of their outlets and introduced new healthier menus in response to criticisms of the company.

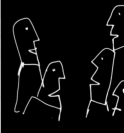

Global food commodities: getting the basics

A visit to any supermarket gives consumers the choice of literally thousands of products, but a closer inspection reveals that many of these are based on the same basic ingredients. These include things such as wheat, maize (corn), rice, sugar, soya and vegetable oils. Together with products such as coffee, cocoa and tea, these are known as commodities and are traded in vast quantities on the global commodity markets everyday.

Global commodity markets

The price paid for food commodities can vary greatly year by year, or even month by month. The graph below shows annual price changes for coffee, but within any year the changes are just as great. In 2008, the monthly price for coffee ranged from 139 cents to 103 cents per pound in weight. This is because the supply and demand is at a global level. A natural disaster such as a flood or hurricane can destroy a country's crop and lead to a shortage in supply and an increase in prices. In 2008, a cyclone destroyed much of the rice crop in Myanmar (Burma), for example, leading experts to warn of increased international prices for rice and causing concerns for countries such as Bangladesh and Sri Lanka that were relying on rice exports from Myanmar.

This graph shows the variation in the price paid for coffee on the world markets. Because coffee growing is a long-term investment for farmers, this variation can make their livelihood very unreliable.

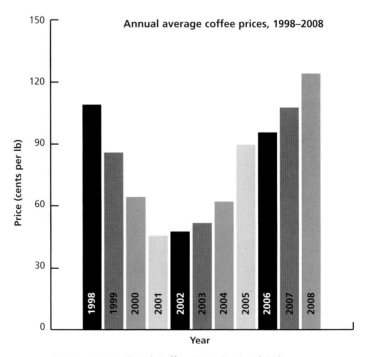

Annual average coffee prices, 1998–2008

Source: International Coffee Organisation (ICO)

Unfair system?

Critics of the global commodity markets complain that they are unfair. They say this is because governments in MDCs provide support for their farmers that governments in LDCs cannot afford to do. They also say that the buying power of large corporations means that they can manipulate the market through their buying choices and cause some farmers to suffer as a result.

Agricultural subsidies

Government support for farmers is normally in the form of subsidies. These are payments that give farmers a guaranteed price for their produce or provide payments even for cultivating the land. The EU gives its farmers around US$50 billion-worth of subsidies per year, and US farmers receive up to US$48 billion per year in various payments. These payments

distort the global commodity markets because some farmers in these regions produce crops based on the payment of subsidies rather than on the market price. Sometimes farmers can be paid more than their produce is actually sold for. This system makes it hard for farmers in countries without subsidies to compete and means that they often get low prices for their produce because the market is flooded with produce from subsidised farms.

Farmers use a machine to harvest rice in South Korea. The South Korean government provides subsidies to its rice farmers, which some global food campaigners believe are unfair. The World Trade Organisation (WTO) is working internationally to try to reduce or eliminate unfair agricultural subsidies.

> *Farmers in countries of the South [LDCs] cannot compete with subsidised agricultural products from Europe. The subsidies the EU pays to farmers in France, Germany, Britain, Spain and elsewhere cheapen European food production in such a way that small farmers in say, Senegal, can no longer exist.*
>
> Thilo Bode, director of Foodwatch, 2009

Cheap products

Agricultural subsidies do much more than affect the income of farmers in LDCs. They can also be linked to changing diets and especially to the global increase in meat consumption, processed foods and obesity. This is because the low price of grains used to feed livestock (corn and soya especially) has kept meat production and meat-based products relatively cheap. Fructose – a common sugar used in many processed foods and drinks – is another product that comes from cheap, subsidised corn. Health experts are now linking our 21st-century culture of fast and processed food directly to these sorts of subsidy payments.

The globalisation of our food industry has led to animals being reared in factory-like conditions, such as this chicken farm in Austria. Many people object to food being produced in this way.

> *Given the popularity of burgers, chicken, and soft drinks in America's fast-food-driven culture, the link between agricultural subsidies, poor diet, and obesity is evident.*
>
> Yale University, Rudd Centre for Food Policy and Obesity, 2008

Buying power

Large food corporations have enormous buying power and can use this to get the best prices for their consumers. This same buying power can distort markets, however. Large buyers can go direct to suppliers instead of buying through the markets. They can negotiate a price that is lower than the market price by guaranteeing to the supplier that they will buy their produce. This can reduce the supply reaching the main market and so cause prices to rise for other buyers (those without the buying power of large corporations).

Some large corporations bypass the market system by owning more stages of the production process, sometimes all the way from farm to plate. The US company Tyson Foods has done this with the supply of chicken. Tyson controls the feed mills, chick hatcheries, slaughterhouses, processing factories and retailing. It pays farmers to rear chickens on the farm, because it is costly to run farms in terms of maintenance, disposal of waste, transportation and so on. However, Tyson insists that farmers buy their food and other inputs, such as medicines, from Tyson.

SPOTLIGHT

Global food crisis

In 2007–2008, the world experienced rapid increases in the price of food. Globally, the price of key food commodities including rice, wheat and maize more than doubled. In many countries this had a dramatic and detrimental effect. Food riots were reported in 36 countries around the world as people struggled to afford to eat. In Haiti, one of the worst-affected places, at least five people were killed during riots and the prime minister was forced to resign. People there had been reduced to eating mud cakes called 'teh', made from mud, margarine and salt, because they could not afford other food following price increases of over 40 per cent.

United Nations peacekeepers try to calm the mood in the capital city of Haiti, following riots over rising food prices in 2008. Five people were killed in the riots, including one UN peacekeeper.

Soya, soya everywhere

Soya is found in an estimated 60–70 per cent of all foods consumed in a modern Western diet, such as that of a UK or US resident. Even the meat we eat is heavily dependent on soya as it makes up the feed given to most mass-produced livestock today. In fact, chicken is so dependent on soya meal that it has been described by some food campaigners as 'soya with feathers'. Like many global food commodities, the soya market is controlled by a few key corporations. In this case, the big three are the US companies Archer Daniels (ADM), Cargill and Bunge, who control virtually everything from the soya seed to the final market.

This aerial image shows soya beans being watered in Brazil. Thousands of hectares of land have been converted to grow soya for the global food industry and the crop is partly blamed for increased rates of deforestation.

> The company [Cargill] grows its own soy on farms... crushes it, moves it within Brazil... imports it into Europe... moves it within the EU to the UK, where it is either then crushed, again by Cargill, or sold forward to Cargill's Sun Valley division, which then feeds it to animals [chickens]... and which are then slaughtered and processed, again by Sun Valley, before being sold [as nuggets].
>
> Raj Patel, author of *Stuffed and Starved*, 2007

A worker shows soya beans from a vast plantation in the Brazilian state of Mato Grosso. The company, Bom Futuro, uses 300 combine harvesters and 500 tractors to produce more than 600,000 tons of soya a year.

Social and environmental impact

The soya bean industry has had major social and environmental impacts around the world, but nowhere more so than in Brazil. Vast areas of forest have been cleared to make way for soya bean farms and small-scale tenant farmers have been thrown off their land by giant commercial farms. Soya is therefore contributing to two of Brazil's greatest challenges – deforestation and landlessness. In Mato Grosso state, at the heart of the Brazilian soya industry, the rate of deforestation has more than doubled in recent years. In Brazil as a whole, the area planted with soya increased from 37,000 hectares in 1971 to over 14 million hectares today – much of it on what was once forest.

The soya in your diet	
Some products containing soya	**Some different names for soya**
Breakfast cereals	Soy
Desserts	Soya flour
Cheeses	Hydrolysed vegetable protein
Soups	Soy protein isolate
Pastries	Protein concentrate
Chocolate	Textured vegetable protein
Sauces	Vegetable oil (hydrogenated or not)
Cakes	Plant sterols
Cereal bars	Lecithin
Gravies	
Noodles	
Sausage casings	
Spreads	

PERSPECTIVES FOR DEBATE

"Most of the land in the Amazon [rainforest] is classed as 'empty' land and is unprotected and vulnerable. Soya farmers target these areas. They use loggers and bulldozers to clear and burn it in readiness of the crop... Soya farming leads to soil erosion, it requires massive chemical inputs to boost harvests. As the soil becomes exhausted farmers move to other areas and repeat the vicious cycle of soil degradation and chemical pollution."

Greenpeace, *Eating up the Amazon*, 2006

"To me, a 40 per cent increase in deforestation doesn't mean anything at all, and I don't feel the slightest guilt over what we are doing here. We are talking about an area larger than Europe that has barely been touched, so there is nothing at all to get worried about."

Blairo Maggi, soya farmer and Governor of Mato Grosso state, Brazil, 2003

The industrialisation and globalisation of the food industry has improved global food supplies to record highs. However, these improvements have not rid the world of hunger, and whilst they may have made food cheaper and more available, there are many who now believe this has come at too high a cost – to the environment, to health, to society, and to cultures. Those who support these views argue that we need to look for alternative models that will build a secure, sustainable and fair food industry for the future.

> *…convenience, low prices and a paradise of choice in supermarkets go hand in hand with price gouging, discrimination, exploitative labour practices, local community destruction, environmental degradation and shiftless profiteering.*

Raj Patel, author of *Stuffed and Starved*, 2007

Rediscovering food

In 2007, a survey of UK children aged 8–15 found that 1 in 50 city children thought pizza came from a farm and over 1 in 20 thought the same of chips. At the same time, around 1 in 7 did not know that carrots or potatoes were produced on farms. Surveys of children in Canada and France have shown similar trends and led many experts to suggest that the global food industry has disconnected us from our food.

Some experts argue that we should be rediscovering food by buying locally produced, seasonal produce rather than the packaged, out-of-season produce sold in our supermarkets. This, they say, would reconnect us to our food by helping us to understand the seasons, support local farmers and rediscover the taste and benefits of fresh food.

> *The food choices you make can impact your local economy, neighbours, province and country. Local food is cheaper and better than imported food, it's fresher for us and helps keep our farms alive.*

Lindsay Babineau, Executive Director, BC Agriculture in the Classroom Foundation, Canada, 2009

SPOTLIGHT

Food miles

One of the most visible signs of the global food industry is the so-called 'food miles', or the distance our food travels. Many campaign groups use this to urge the food industry to change and to highlight the relationship between the global food industry and climate change. As consumers, it might be easy to decide whether or not to buy strawberries flown in from the other side of the world, but what about more complicated processed foods? The map below, for example, shows the possible ingredients and food miles of a typical take-out pizza sold in the UK.

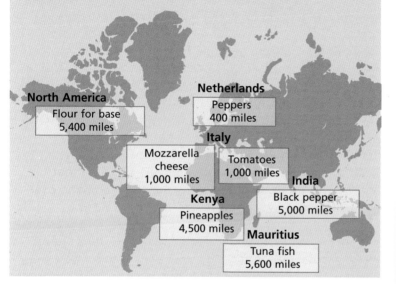

North America
Flour for base
5,400 miles

Netherlands
Peppers
400 miles

Italy
Mozzarella cheese
1,000 miles

Tomatoes
1,000 miles

India
Black pepper
5,000 miles

Kenya
Pineapples
4,500 miles

Mauritius
Tuna fish
5,600 miles

Local farmers' markets, such as this one in Berlin, sell locally produced and seasonal foods and have been increasing in popularity in recent years as people reject supermarkets and return to a more locally based diet.

Working with nature

The intensive farming practices that lie behind the modern global food industry are heavily reliant on fertilisers, pesticides, herbicides and other chemical inputs, but these can have negative impacts on the environment and on human health. Some agricultural chemicals have been linked to birth defects and increased rates of cancer.

Organic agriculture is a system of farming practices that avoids the use of such chemicals and instead tries to work with nature by mixing crops that naturally fertilise the land or have properties that deter pests and diseases. Supporters of organic food also point out that it does not carry the same health risks as conventional farming. The amount of land under organic farming worldwide has increased considerably in recent years, as have the sales of organic food. The Soil Association, which monitors sales of organic food in the UK, reported that sales topped £2 billion for the first time in 2006 – a figure 22 per cent higher than in the previous year. Sales in the USA have also grown and were around US$20 billion in 2007, compared to less than US$1 billion in 1990. Despite such impressive increases, organic sales showed signs of falling during 2008 because of rising world food prices and consumers turning to cheaper, conventional produce.

A Soil Association bag promotes one of the reasons it believes organic food is becoming more popular with consumers. People want to know their food is produced naturally and safely and the Soil Association will only allow companies that meet strict standards to use their brand.

SPOTLIGHT

Grow your own

At one time, growing your own food was relatively common, but supermarkets and convenience changed that. Today, as people seek alternatives to the global industry, growing your own food has again become popular. Allotments are in high demand and are sometimes run as cooperatives with several people sharing the labour and cost of a plot and the food it produces. Even city dwellers have managed to find small areas of land to convert into food-producing gardens and urban farming is a fast-growing source of locally produced food in many countries.

A woman harvests produce from a community allotment in Seattle, USA. Growing your own food has become increasingly popular in recent years in many MDCs.

Making it fair

One of the biggest criticisms of the global food industry is that it has allowed the large food corporations to dominate and trade in ways that are unfair to many of those involved. Many farmers find themselves unable to earn a living because they are being paid constantly lower prices for their produce. An alternative to this is fair trade. Fair trade provides farmers with guaranteed prices for their produce that are higher than the average market price. The farmers are told what they will be paid before they plant, and are normally paid some of their money in advance. This allows them to plan their growing with greater confidence and means they can afford to invest in the growth of their farms and the future of their families.

Increasing fair trade

There are a growing number of fair trade products (see below) available to consumers in countries with a fair trade scheme. To qualify as a fair trade product and carry the fair trade logo, suppliers must meet certain standards such as paying a fair price and respecting workers' rights and the environment.

SPOTLIGHT

Fair trade products

These are some of the more popular fair trade food products that are now widely available in many MDCs:

Coffee	Tea	Chocolate	Bananas	Honey
Sugar	Fruit juices	Fruits and jams	Wine	Rice

The fair trade movement now has schemes operating in 23 countries and by 2008 was supporting 632 producer organisations, representing some 7.5 million farming families across 58 countries.

Making fair trade fairer: nuts

Nuts are a relatively small part of total fair trade food and are only now starting to be sold in some countries. In the UK, one nut company called Liberation is taking fair trade for farmers even further than the standards set by the Fairtrade Labelling Organisation. They have developed a system (see diagram opposite) that has fewer stages between the growers and the end consumers so that more of the profits make their way back to the growers. The 22,000 growers who are spread across Nicaragua, Peru, Brazil, Bolivia, Mozambique, Malawi, and Kerala in Southern India own 42 per cent of the company, which means they benefit as growers from every single sale that is made.

> *[Liberation] takes fair trade to the next stage, bringing producers right up the supply chain, replacing the last link, the importer, through a farmer-owned brand, which empowers smallholder producers by involving them in ALL decisions taken and maximising THEIR profits. Through Liberation's supply chain, farmers sell DIRECTLY to the retailers in Europe.*

Liberation website, 2009

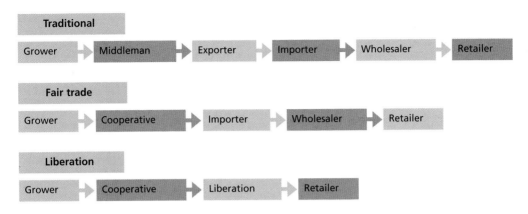

Traditional

Grower → Middleman → Exporter → Importer → Wholesaler → Retailer

Fair trade

Grower → Cooperative → Importer → Wholesaler → Retailer

Liberation

Grower → Cooperative → Liberation → Retailer

This diagram compares traditional and fair trade systems of nut production with the Liberation system.

> *I am from Fairtrade Alliance Kerala (FTAK) and we produce Fairtrade cashew nuts for Liberation. Owning this new company is tremendously encouraging and motivating for our farmers. The farmers tell each other: 'We are selling to ourselves! We cannot ever compromise on quality.' This new nut company is symbolic that the farmers have hope. This is about farmers' organisations coming together.*
>
> FTAK member, Kerala, 2009

Processing Brazil nuts is a labour-intensive task. Fair trade companies ensure that workers receive fair treatment and a greater share of the profits.

Becoming an active global citizen

What is an active global citizen? It is someone who tries, in their own small way, to make the world a better place. To become an active global citizen, you will need to get involved in decisions that others make about your life and the lives of others around the world. Consider how the world could be changed, such as improving the environment, political or social conditions for others, and seek information about the issues from a wide variety of sources. Then go public by presenting your arguments to others, from classmates and local groups, to national politicians and global organisations.

In your life

Many of us take the food we eat for granted and give little thought to how it connects us to a massive global industry. And yet, that food or drink has often travelled thousands of miles and passed from company to company before it ends up on our table. The activities below suggest some ways that you could begin to become more connected to the food in your life.

Keep a food diary. Make a note of the food you eat in a day or week and try to identify where the different items come from. How many countries does your diet connect you with? What are the most surprising results? To show your global diet visually, mark the origins of your food on a blank world map, downloaded from a site such as http://www.eduplace.com/ss/maps/world.html.

Be supermarket aware. Next time you visit a supermarket, see how many food products have an organic or fair trade alternative. How much more would it cost you to buy these alternatives? Is that a price you are willing to pay? Could you buy the food your household consumes without visiting a large supermarket? What sort of things cannot be bought locally?

Notice adverts. Consider the food products (including drinks) that are advertised on TV or in magazines around your home. What sort of products are advertised the most? How do you think advertising can influence diets?

Notice choice. Next time you visit a large town or city near you, look at how many different styles of food are available to choose from. If you can't visit a place then you could try using the internet to do a search for restaurants in a town or city. Share what you have found with your parents or grandparents. How has the choice of food changed since they were your age?

Grow your own. Find out what food you could grow yourself. Local libraries and the internet can be good places to find out what you would need and how to get started. Remember that you don't always need much space, so everyone should be able to grow something.

Key terms for internet searches

Type these terms into a search engine on the internet and see what results you get. How many hits appear? Are the websites from around the world, and are there any information sources that surprise you?

- Climate change and food
- Fair trade food
- Farmers' markets
- Farming subsidies
- Fast food
- Food and biofuels
- Food miles
- Food prices
- Food waste
- Grow your own food
- Healthy eating
- Local food
- Malnutrition
- Obesity
- Organic food
- Supermarket power
- Virtual water
- Food commodities

Data watch

The following websites can help you to keep up to date with statistics and information relating to the global food industry.

http://www.fairtrade.org.uk/products/default.aspx has information about the range of fair trade food products available to buy.

http://www.soilassociation.org/library is packed with information about organic food and farming. Use the search function on the site to find what you are looking for.

Visit the International Food Policy Research Institute at http://www.ifpri.org for information about the battle to end world hunger and poverty. It includes the interactive Global Hunger Index – a map that shows which countries have the greatest hunger problems.

Use the internet to monitor the price of a major food commodity over time. Coffee prices can be found at http://www.ico.org/coffee_prices.asp

http://www.worldmapper.org
What is different about the maps on this site is that countries and regions are distorted according to the data. Here are a few maps to explore: 47) Cereals exports; 53) Groceries exports; 54) Groceries imports; 178) Undernourishment; 363) International food aid; 364) International fast food; 451) Cardiovascular (heart and blood vessel) disease.

http://www.worldometers.info
Ever wanted to see the rate at which data such as world population or the number of internet users change? This website has up-to-the-minute information! See the food section for fast-changing figures on food production, obesity and undernourishment.

Topic web

Use this topic web to discover the themes and ideas in subject areas related to the food industry.

Geography
Explore different models of farming from around the world and consider the positive and negative aspects of each model. Make a list of the factors that cause them to vary.

Citizenship
Produce a leaflet to inform shoppers about fair trade foods and their link with poverty reduction in LDCs. What will you tell them? Think about the sort of language and presentation you might use. What images do you need to support your leaflet?

English
Write a poem to describe your favourite meal to someone you have never met. Think about all of the flavours, smells, shapes and colours that can be found in your meal and try to build in something about where it has come from and how it was made.

Maths
Take a typical shop-bought meal, such as a pizza, and work out the food miles for each ingredient. Now research the average price of each ingredient if they were to be purchased separately. Using the two sets of figures, calculate the approximate cost per mile for each ingredient to work out which is the most expensive in food mile terms.

The Food Industry

History
Find out about some of the great famine events of the past (eg Ireland, China, Ethiopia) and consider what caused them. What lessons can be learnt for avoiding famines in the future?

PE
Find out which foods are good for improving performance in different sports. You might consider strength, stamina, speed and agility.

ICT
Investigate how much of your diet could be met by shopping using the internet. How easy is it to buy food on the internet? How quick is it? How would you improve the sites you visit? What are the pros and cons of internet shopping for food?

Science
Investigate the science of genetic modification (GM) and how it is being used in the food industry. Make a list of scientific questions that you would like to put to a GM food expert.

Glossary

biodiversity The range of plants and animals living in a particular habitat.

boycott A form of protest that normally involves refusing to trade with certain companies, countries or people.

brand A symbol, mark or quality that characterises a product.

brand bombing When a company uses its superior wealth and power to bring its brand into new markets.

buying power The power that an individual or company has as a buyer, compared to others in the market. If you have greater wealth or want to buy more of something, you normally have greater buying power.

calorie A measure of the energy contained in food. All food can be measured in calories, and levels of hunger are measured by how many calories we consume in a day.

climate change Significant changes in the world's climate, including temperature and weather patterns. Some people believe this is linked to human activity such as carbon emissions into the atmosphere.

commodity An item that is traded as a raw material in the global markets. In the food industry, commodities include sugar, coffee, tea, soya, wheat, rice and cocoa.

consumption The purchasing of goods and services for use.

cooperative A system in which people join up to share the costs, labour, risks and benefits of producing something.

corporate Business-related.

exploitative Using human labour for the benefit of a company or organisation without giving fair return such as wages, decent working conditions and benefits.

franchising A system that allows businesses to expand by local people setting up a local business that sells their brand and product. Many fast food companies use franchising.

greenhouse gases Atmospheric gases, such as carbon dioxide, methane, nitrous oxide and water vapour, which contribute to the greenhouse effect that is warming the planet.

industrialisation The process by which something becomes organised like an industry. Increased use of machinery and external inputs (chemicals, etc) has made the food industry increasingly industrialised.

intensive farming A system of farming that seeks to maximise the amount of crops or animals produced, often by using chemicals to boost production.

interdependent When organisations, industries or individuals are mutually dependent on each other to make something work.

less developed countries (LDCs) Countries that have a lower income and poorer standards in health, nutrition, education and industry than more developed countries (MDCs).

media All means of providing or communicating information to the public, including radio, the internet, television, mobile phones and newspapers.

migrate To move from one country or region to settle in another.

more developed countries (MDCs) Countries that have a higher income and better standards in health, nutrition, education and industry than less developed countries (LDCs).

multi-cultural Sharing elements of many different cultures. Most large cities are multi-cultural because of the wide range of people living there.

obesity A condition in which people are extremely, often dangerously, overweight. It is normally caused by poor diet and lack of exercise.

organic Produced without the use of artificial chemicals such as pesticides on crops or routine drugs for farm animals.

pesticides Chemicals used in agriculture to prevent crops being affected by insect or weed pests.

subsidies Payments made to an industry by its government.

sustainable Able to be maintained at a steady level for a long time, without causing environmental or social damage.

transnational company (TNC) A company that operates across several nations.

United Nations (UN) A group of 192 member states that works globally in many areas, including peace, international law, health, education and human rights.

World Health Organisation (WHO) An organisation of the United Nations, concerned with worldwide public health.

World Trade Organisation (WTO) An organisation that deals with global rules of trade.

Index